Contrasts
Nuts and bolts

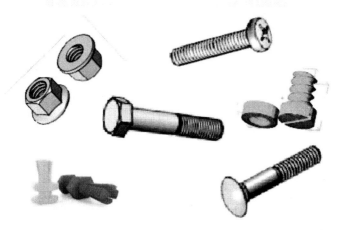

A Plateau Area Writers
Association Anthology

Contrasts
Nuts and bolts

A Plateau Area Writers
Association Anthology

Contrasts is an anthology publication of the Plateau Area Writers Association of aspiring and accomplished authors in communities of South King and North Pierce Counties bordering the foothills of the Cascade Mountains in the state of Washington and seven other states.

Paul T. Jackson, Editor

© 2016 Plateau Area Writers Association
P.O. Box 1974
Buckley, WA 98321
http://plateauareawriters.org/
pawainfo@comcast.net

All rights reserved. No portion may be reproduced by any means without permission.
Authors own their own copyrights.

ISSN 2332-0338

DEDICATION

PAWA is blessed by the wisdom of our older members, and we need to keep them in our prayers as we go forward. Some keep going on even with frailties of body, sight, and disease. They are all dealing with the nuts and bolts of living, but with the additional issues of health.

With grateful recognition of those efforts we dedicate this issue.

CONTENTS

Authors	Titles	pages
Wendy N. Bell	Nuts and Bolts of Poetrics	31
Miriam A. Bowers	A Three Penny Nut	8-10
A. Louise Deffley	A Sudden Storm	11-26
Marjorie Eldred	Nuts and Bolts	10
	The Nuts and I	32-33
	The Nut and the Beauty Salon	38-39
Robert S. Gaylord	It May be English, but—	34-35
	Texas Education: The King Ranch	46-49
Jeanette Hallock	A Personal Obituary	61
Diana Harbeck	What makes a woman Beautiful	27
Isabel Jackson	Long Lake - July	60
	Long Lake Musings	64
JoAnn Lakin Jackson	Sort Of will Never Do	52-60
Paul T. Jackson	Critic's Corner	42-44
Alan C. Keimig	The Machinery Turn Into Life	41
	Working to Preserve	45
	Who We Do Become	49
Kenneth S. Lapham	Reflected Consideration	33
Marilyn White	Nuts and Bolts of my Dad	36-37
	Build up of the cheeseburger	50-51
	Nuts and Bolts of Writing a Villanelle	65-67
Phyllis Bjork Williams	Rain pastiche	28-29
	Memoir Baking	62-63

Foreword:

The Plateau Area Writers Association (PAWA) members have been producing two publications since 2002. These are a Quarterly and a themed Anthology. The latter has had many titles, until 2010 when the work became an annual publication under a series title, *Contrasts*.

1. 2002 Remember
2. 2003 PAWA Full Fiction
3. 2003 We Were Young Once
4. 2004 Winter Stories
5. 2005 Unexpected Heroes
6. 2006 Reigning Cats and Dogs
7. 2006 Celebrations
8. 2007 Fact, Fiction or Farce
9. 2007 Defining Moments
10. 2008 Scary Moments
11. 2008 Potpourri
12. 2009 Sweet Dreams and Nightmares
13. 2009 Stories for Young Readers
14. 2010 Magical Moments; Unexplained Events
15. 2010 CONTRASTS: Apples and Oranges
16. 2011 CONTRASTS: Guilt or Innocence
17. 2012 CONTRASTS: More or Less
18. 2013 CONTRASTS: Coffee or Tea
19. 2014 CONTRASTS: Before and After
20. 2015 CONTRASTS: Here and/or There
21. 2016 CONTRASTS: Nuts and Bolts

The *Plateau Area Writers Quarterly* began as an eight-page newsletter in 1999, with member contributions, and has grown to a twenty-page publication including Meetings' Program speakers, President's Corner, information about critique, creative groups, and member activity. There are stories, memoirs, and poems written by members ranging in age from middle school to 90s. We encourage you to join us as a writer, as a subscriber, or an advertiser. The Quarterly is available electronically to libraries through EBSCOhost.

-- Paul T. Jackson, Editor

A Three-Penny Nut
© April 30, 2016, by Miriam A. Bowers

When we first began our heavy construction business, we bought used equipment from auctions. These worn-out loaders and backhoes were frequently in need of repair as we carried out our first jobs of sewer hook-ups. Tony, my husband, was a good mechanic. However, repairs took too much of his time, and as he took on bigger jobs, repairs needed more time than he could spare, and idle equipment made laborers idle. They got paid for time on the job site, even if they did no work. Sending the workers home raised another problem. Once an employer found a good worker, he wanted to keep him on the job. Otherwise, he would be hired away, and the employer would be sent someone else, who most likely would be a slacker.

What to do? Reputable repair shops cost too much money for us.

The answer seemed be to send the equipment to a community college nearby where mechanics were in training. The turnaround time would be greater, but the equipment would be fixed, and, under the eyes of the instructor, the repairs would be done properly.

The next time the backhoe/loader broke down we sent it to the local community college. During the time the equipment was gone, Tony kept his laborers doing jobs manually, which could be done faster with equipment, or they did "fill-in jobs", those he would have them do during downtime. When, at last, the backhoe/loader was returned, it worked fine for a few hours, but by the end of the day it broke down again.

After sending the workers home, Tony spent a few hours looking into the machinery for the trouble. At last, he found it. He groaned. It was a missing nut on a bolt. He felt outraged; someone had left off, or failed to secure a nut on a bolt, a three-cent part. He thought of what it had cost him: another repair job, the cost not only for the hours wasted of the workers' time, but also of the damage to the backhoe/loader caused by the missing bolt and nut. His anger grew. He thought of the supposedly lower price of the unsatisfactory repair.

He regretted sending the backhoe/loader to unskilled repairmen. After this, he would have to bear the price of sending equipment to a regular shop, or do it himself. He lacked the proper lift and pit, but he could weld and construct a hoist during the next break between jobs. It was too costly to stop the current job. He'd have to do the repair on-site and use manpower in place of a shop hoist.

The next day he sent an order for two of his best and strongest workers. The rest went to other jobs. He set the two men up to add their weight to the counterweights on the equipment. Enough lift was gained to elevate the arm of the loader into the air. He propped a wooden piece of lumber to hold the arm in place.

He began to work on the repair. He was almost done, when one of the laborers began to tire of their strained position and shifted his weight. The prop slipped away, and the loader arm came down. Tony's finger was between two metal plates that slid past each other and very neatly sliced off the tip of his finger. Although it was a clean cut, it was a greasy wound and bleeding profusely. In shock, the quickest of the workers to react told Tony he would drive him to the nearest emergency room. Seeing how badly the finger was bleeding, Tony was convinced and agreed. He sent the other worker home. They drove to the university hospital nearby and presented Tony's finger and tip to be sewed back in place.

The surgeon present at the time was a teaching professor. He shook his head. He was visibly delighted to see before him a repair example to show students and demonstrate to his interns how the repair should be done, reconnecting blood vessels, etc. He refused the proffered tip as unsanitary and, in operating, formed a tent-like structure of strips of skin and flesh and sutured them together.

Of course, a demonstration to the students had to be more

elaborate than an army field operation, and had to be appropriately expensive. Tony called that finger, "Goldfinger", ever after that incident.

    Tony progressively bid on bigger and bigger jobs. Finally, we were able to buy a new, not used, big backhoe after several years of feast and famine. It cost as much as our house.

Nuts and Bolts

I'm supposed to write on nuts and bolts
Or bolts and nuts; my mind is shut.
Of ideas, it's completely blank
Of nuts I've known or thoughts I've 'thank'.
The 'nuts' I've known I can't remember
A thing they've done since last September.
Of putting nuts on a bolt or a screw,
Well that's a thing I just don't do.
So, sorry guys, my mind is stuck;
Anthology's just out of luck.

© 2016, By Marjorie Eldred

A SUDDEN STORM
©July 10, 2016, Louise Deffley

Following a week of rain, this Thursday turned out to be a perfect spring day. There was reason to hope it would continue. Only this morning the weatherman on Channel Five had promised three or more days of sunshine to come.

Since it was a Thursday, the Black Diamond museum was open to the public. Childish laughter rang out from a group of school children on a field trip to learn about local history. Several of the boys were investigating the old locomotive out front. That locomotive was all that remained to remind people that at one time trains actually steamed into Black Diamond.

Across the street, Mike's Pizzeria and Deli was open for business. Next to the museum, the fragrance of coffee drifted from the Baker Street Bookstore. Most everyone knew that Bob kept fresh coffee available for his patrons.

Thanks to Bob's hospitality, the bookstore had become similar to an old county store, one where neighbors gathered to visit a bit. After all, the building was once the Company Store for the coal mine workers. After that, it was the local tavern; all places where friendly people just naturally gather.

It was indeed a pleasant day for those coming and going. Happy in the sunshine, no one noticed the fairly brisk breeze ruffling the flag at the corner by the museum.

The Baker Street bookstore was enjoying a somewhat busy day. Among others, Sara O'Brien had brought her four grandchildren for a visit. The small parking area was full of cars. Tom, from the museum stopped in for a quick cup of coffee. He couldn't linger for a visit since there were too many children wishing to climb all over the old locomotive. Mostly that was allowed - but not too many at once.

Bob, the owner of Baker Street Books, was enjoying the day. Although if he thought of it he might remember the long evening ahead. The ladies' Thursday night book club would be in at seven.

Just before seven o'clock, Bob stepped outside and swept the days traffic from the porch. He didn't look up to notice the narrow dark cloud forming just north of Railroad Avenue, or the brisk breeze that swept along the avenue. Perhaps he had noted the full moon just showing in the east when the ladies arrived.

Two hours later, at nine o'clock, dark clouds were now racing across the sky, partially hiding the full moon. A sharp wind was whipping sheets of rain across the street.

One lady called out, "Man it's wet out here. The weatherman was sure wrong."

Voices could be heard shouting their goodbyes, as car doors slammed shut:

"See you next week."

"My goodness it is wet out here. The weatherman sure goofed."

"Drive safely now."

Bob stood at the door to make sure all went well. Rain was coming in a downpour, wind driven almost sideways on to the covered porch.

Bob breathed a sigh of relief so deep it seemed to echo down the street. He was quick to close the door. Before he turned the key in the lock, he glanced at the posters on the inside of his door. That let him knew he was truly closed for the night.

He enjoyed having the ladies' book review group make use of his bookstore. Nevertheless, at times it seemed to extend his day a bit too long. This was true, especially on nights when he had a load of books to catalog and shelf. Tomorrow night would also be a late one. He would be open until ten o'clock for the jazz night he enjoyed.

For a moment he stood there, a tall man just over six feet, his pleasant face set in a frown. He ran his fingers through his thick brown hair and sighed once again.

Mumbling to himself, "Get with it Bob. It's already a bit after nine."

He rounded the counter and looked through the rain-stained glass to see only darkness filling the street. Not even a gleam of light filtered from the windows of the stately old building across the street.

Railroad Avenue, he thought, *perhaps once there was a train station here, but now there is only a museum to mark the spot where trains squeaked to a stop way back in the early nineteen hundreds.*

He pushed up the sleeves of his warm flannel shirt and turned his attention to the stack of books covering the sturdy counter. For some reason, he once again leaned toward the window, drawn by the sound of heavy rainfall and a whistling wind. It certainly looked lonely out there tonight.

"It is a miserable night out." He uttered out loud. "Bob, better get with it. There is too much to accomplish before I can head for home. I must be out of my mind. Still, in all, tomorrow could easily be a busy day. I hope!"

Then he smiled to himself and thought, *I must be getting old talking out loud to myself that way.*

"Coffee, that's what I need."

Shaking his head at his outspoken remark, he turned his hand to making a fresh pot of brew to help keep his wits about him this stormy night.

Soon the fragrant scent of coffee filled the building, blending with the lilting sound of a Scottish tune. He felt a sense of well-being in spite of the weather. Wind rattled the windows. A distant rumble of thunder filled the building. When he looked out again, he saw several small flashes of lightning toward the north. Just then, a flash of light filled the old building. Bob quickly opened the door to look outside. North of Railroad Avenue he saw a long, jagged bolt of lightning. Quickly it was

13

followed by yet another. His ears ached from the following thunder. He stepped outside to be brought to a standstill by a jolting, loud clap of thunder. The building shook. There was a strange green and yellow glow in the sky. In fact, everything was reflecting that weird color. As he stepped back inside, he noted a faint glimmer of it also filled the store.

"Wow! That was close." Bob exclaimed.

His ears were ringing and he felt a buzz of energy rush through him. He titled his head to the side, and listened to the sound of rain pelting the windows on the museum side of the building.

Bob shook his head. He thought he heard a train whistle. That couldn't be. This storm and the lateness of the hour were getting to him.

"It must have been nothing but the wind playing a tune."

He reassured himself. It was simply not possible for a train to come into Black Diamond. There were no longer any tracks.

He crossed over to stand by the window. Outside he could see the area continued to glow with the same weird sort of greenish light that still filled his store.

"Wonder what caused that?" He questioned the air. "Strange! In fact very strange!"

Turning from the window, he felt relieved his lights were still on.

"Get busy Bob." He resumed his way about the shelves. Then he slowed his steps to listen. Shaking his head, he knew that was not a horse and wagon he had heard.

Quickly he turned once again to his work. Then, he paused again to listen. He wasn't sure. Was that a tapping at his door?

I'm losing it. My imagination is working over time. Looking at his watch he discovered it was almost midnight. He realized he had been so absorbed in his task, he had forgotten the time. He had been at it for about three hours. He couldn't believe it. It was time to go home.

14

Just then a sharp tapping interrupted his thoughts. It sounded louder this time. It sounded somewhat urgent.
"Who in the devil would be at my door this time of night in that mess outside?"
He was once again hearing his own voice.
He hurried to unlock the door. Cautiously he peeked around the edge of the door to see just who or what was outside. There stood a slightly-built woman with her hand raised up to rap again on the sturdy door. She had one hand ready to knock. Her other hand held a huge black umbrella. She made quite a picture.
Her face was settled into a determined look. Bob could see that, although her face was almost obscured by a very wet black felt hat. It draped over her head almost hiding her eyes. Desperation and fatigue radiated from her.
Seeing him, she tilted her head to look up.
Softly, she asked, "What is this place?"
"Why, it's a bookstore." He hurriedly answered, adding. "Come in here out of that storm. It is far too late, way too dark and damp for anyone to be outside tonight."
He opened the door wider and stood aside for her to enter.
Before she stepped inside, she turned and shook out her umbrella and folded it up. Then she turned to pick up her large satchel.
"Here, let me get that."
Bob hurried to step around her. He stared down at the enormous bag. It appeared to be made of rose-colored floor carpet. There were handles of leather firmly attached to the sides. When he lifted it, he couldn't believe this petite woman had carried it.
Setting the heavy bag inside, he reached for the dripping umbrella. Bob hurried to place it in the antique umbrella stand that stood in one corner of the counter. He thanked his good fortune for having obtained it just a few months before. The umbrella looked at home there. He noted somehow the woman

15

looked at home also. Her clothing was from another era, just how far back he wasn't sure. Not being up on women's fashions over the years, he only knew it certainly was not today's style. Regardless of age most women of the twenty-first century didn't wear dresses down to the ankles. She also wore a long, black woolen coat over it all.

"Come over here by the stove so you can warm up."

She hesitated, turning to look about her. She was still obviously puzzled.

"What is this place?" She asked again. "I was told this was the Company Store. I was leery of coming here. It may not have been open. But, you see I am so tired and worried. I didn't know what else to do."

She continued to stand like a deer frozen in the headlights of a car. Her grey eyes were wide and anxious.

"Don't worry, there's nothing but books here. No one is going to harm you. This is my place." He hastened to tell her. "Now just let me take your coat and hat."

Bob helped her off with her damp coat. He couldn't help looking at her with questions in his eyes. He realized it would take some time before answers would be forthcoming.

Finally, she decided to settle down into the tall-backed rocker that was always beside the cheerful stove.

It was then he saw her shoes were high-topped and buttoned all the way up the front.

Noticing his eyes on her feet, she tucked them under the chair and tugged at her long skirts to be sure her ankles were covered. With her gesture of propriety, a feeling of helplessness came upon him. Just what was he to do with this woman?

Who was she? Where had she come from on such a night as this? He supposed he'd have to ask her. Bob didn't enjoy asking personal questions of anyone. However, he guessed he had better start.

"My name is Bob. Usually I'm not open this time of night, but tonight I've been busy getting ready for tomorrow."

16

He paused. "Do you mind giving me your name and letting me know just how you came to knock on my door this night?"

"He didn't come." She covered her face in her hands. "He wasn't there to meet the train. He promised!" Her shoulders shook. Tears found their way down her cheeks.

"I am so worried."

Bob stared at her. "Who didn't come?" He asked.

Blotting her tears with a man's white handkerchief, she placed her hands in her lap and answered.

"John, my son. He promised if I came he would be here to meet me. I've come a very long way."

She looked up into Bob's face with a frown.

"What do you supposed has happened to him?"

Bob leaned over and patted her shoulder. He was more puzzled now than ever. Something must be done, but what?

"Coffee; maybe you'd like some hot coffee. I made a pot just a while ago." He paused. "It's still fresh and hot. It could help warm you up. Maybe then we can think of what to do."

Twisting the handkerchief between nervous fingers, she tried a little smile.

"Why that would be nice of you. Cream and sugar, if you have it would also be nice. Oh, I do have a letter from John. Let me show you."

Busying himself with finding the nicest mug he had in the shop, Bob filled the cup, sweetened and added the powered milk he kept around for those who like that sort of thing. He frowned to himself and found it impossible to remove the inquiring look from his face when he handed her the cup.

"Maybe I could see your letter. It may help decide what to do."

He still wasn't sure just how to handle this situation. He had better get started.

"Madam, could you please tell me your name. It could be that I know your son. Many people come into my shop to buy books. I do know most of the people here abouts."

He tried to be patient. It wasn't easy.

"I'm Mrs. Etta May Samuelson. My son is John M. Samuelson. The M stands for Matthew after his father, God rest his soul. After I wrote him about his father, Matthew, dying, leaving me a widow without much to live on, John wrote me to come here to Black Diamond, Washington."

She paused to sip her coffee with a sigh of pleasure.

"It took all the money I had left to purchase my ticket here from Virginia. John told me not to worry, since he had a good job in the coal mines around here."

Slowly she began to rock the chair back and forth. She held the mug of warmth close to her body. Her head was beginning to nod a little. Her eyes fluttered close and she softly gave a little sigh.

Bob began to notice how pale she looked. There was a faint halo surrounding her entire body. He supposed it was from the floor lamp behind her chair. It gave her something more than a 3-D image. *It's my imagination,* he thought and shook his head a bit. He couldn't let her fall asleep in that chair. What to do?

Seating himself in the upholstered chair across from her, he studied her face. She was far from young, but certainly not elderly. His mother had been about that age when they lost her to cancer. This woman's face held the same gentle look his mother's had. There were smile lines etched around her mouth. Laughter wrinkles radiated from the corners of her eyes. Although the grey eyes flecked with green held a world of sadness and weariness, they were clear and alert. The abundant, dark-brown hair framing her face was streaked with silver. She wore it caught up into an old-fashioned bun at the back of her head.

As he watched her, he found himself being drawn to whatever problem she had. Still, what was he to do with her? His dad was home alone on such a night. There were just the two of them now. Bob did not like to have him worry. Somehow he would have to resolve this dilemma and get home to his dad.

The sound of her coffee mug hitting the hearth jerked him back to the moment at hand. The lady was asleep in the rocker. Her head rested against the wide curve of the back. Her hands were now motionless in her lap. The sound of soft, whisper-like snores left no doubt that Mrs. Samuelson was asleep. Even the clatter of the falling cup had not awakened her.

She must be very tired. Exhausted would probably be the word to use were I talking out loud. I'll have to deal with this somehow. But how?

Bob picked up the mug noticing there had been no coffee left to spill on his hearth. *Asleep, she's asleep. What shall I do with her?* Putting the cup down beside his coffee pot, he walked back through the bookstore checking out the windows. He peeked out each one to see if there was anything or anyone outside. Nothing! No movement; he could see there was only the streetlights casting a shimmer over the wet pavement.

Bob pondered: *Well, I have these couches here. Why not settled her onto one and let her sleep for the night. Yes, why not.*

Coming to a decision, he quickly acted upon it. Walking briskly back to where she slept, he gently touched Mrs. Samuelson's shoulder, shaking it slightly. She looked up at him through half-closed eyes.

"You've come a long way tonight. I know you've had a disappointment. There is really nothing we can do until the morning. I have to get home to my dad."

He paused to be sure she was listening. She nodded her head, sleep heavy in her eyes.

"There is a comfortable couch in the back where you can rest for the remainder of the night. There is a ladies' room, if you have the need and a thick blanket of fine Scottish wool to keep you warm."

He took one of her hands tentatively, pulling her up. He led her down the short hall to the ladies room. Turning on the light, he told her,

"I'll be just over by the stove when you are ready to rest. Don't be embarrassed or fearful. No harm can come to you here. I promise."

It seemed a long minute before she reappeared in front of him. She had unfastened her hair; the dark, silver streaked strands now hung in braids on either side of her face.

Looking up at him, she said, "Somehow I feel I can trust you. I believe I'm ready to rest now. I do feel refreshed but ever so weary. I am not sure I could walk another step. If you could bring my bag, I have something to give you."

A slight smile curved her lips, as she followed him to the back where the couch waited. She sat down and waited for her bag.

Bob put it down close to the couch. Mrs. Samuelson reached inside to bring out a brown paper bag. It rattled a little when she placed it on the bed.

"Mr. Charles, I brought these pecans from the trees in my yard. John loves them. He had written he couldn't find any of these nuts around here. I want to share them with you. Do you have a bowl?"

Bob was surprised. Pecans were readily available in most stores. Then he thought, maybe once they were not.

"Yes, I'll get one." Off he went to find a bowl. Fortunately he had a small one a customer had made at the local pottery shop. Returning, he went to his guest.

She took the bowl and filled it with the nuts. As she handed the bowl back to Bob, she remarked, "These are what we call paper shell pecans. You can just crack them with your fingers. Not all pecans are that easy."

"Thank you very much. I do like pecans. I hope John won't mind."

His guest only smiled and yawned.

Finally, she was settled. He looked down on her as a faint "thank you" drifted his way. He covered her with one of the plaid blankets he carried for sale.

Well, he thought, *what better use than to comfort a deserted lady.* Arms folded over his chest, Bob stood watching her until he was certain she was fast asleep. The gentle rise and fall of the blanket plus the same soft whistling snore he had heard before convinced him she was down for the remainder of the night. She seemed to be from another time, or another world. There was just something about the way she appeared to be surrounded by a mist that puzzled him. Shaking his head, pulling his hands over his eyes he thought I'm *just tired. My eyes are strained from the work of the day. This is crazy; Forget it Bob, and go on home.*

With that thought, he quietly tiptoed his way to his coat and out the door into the wet night. Looking up into the boiling clouds, backlit by what seemed to be constant small bolts of lightning he said out loud,

"What a night! Oh my! What a night!"

All the way home he thought of the little lady he had left

behind. His thoughts also raced ahead to his dad and what was left of his own night. Checking his rear view mirror, he thought he saw a startling flare of lightning off to the northwest. It was bright, lighting up the sky all around Black Diamond.

Strange, he thought, *there was no thunder to be heard that time.* All the way home his thoughts twisted between the woman asleep in his store and his own desire for sleep.

As Bob's car headed south, back in Black Diamond Sid Goldsmith experienced something strange. Sid lived on Railroad Avenue north of the bookstore. He was just crawling back into bed after a necessary night trip to his bathroom. The brightness of the lightning strike Bob had observed in his rearview mirror lit up Sid's bedroom bright as day.

21

An eerie green glow filled the room. His entire body tingled as if he had put his finger in a light socket.

"Whoa!" He said. "That was a close one. But that's not thunder I hear is it? It sounds more like horses hoofs."

Going to the window he looked out down the street toward the cemetery where he believed the light and sound had come from.

"Did you hear that? Joan, are you awake?"

He nudged his sleeping wife. She just turned over and settled in again as if she had not heard him. Turning his head from side to side to hear better, he could swear he heard something like a wagon rattling down the street. It had been years since he had heard such a sound on this road.

Somehow he felt displaced. Air seemed to whirl about him; he was tingling and numb. He felt the hair on his head and neck prickle. He pushed his fingers through it smoothing it down.

"This won't do." He mumbled under his breath.

"Something is very wrong outside."

Walking softly so as not to disturb Joan, he made his way downstairs. He slipped into his rubber boots, pulled a raincoat on over his pajamas and jammed his old slouch hat over his tousled gray hair. Cautiously opening his front door, he stepped out onto his porch.

The night silence was pierced by a loud shrieking noise. Sid hesitated. He couldn't believe what he was hearing much less what he was seeing. It was like looking at a movie set in his own front yard and street. He stepped off his porch and felt the rain mist into his face.

Although he was shaking now, he seemed to know he was outside of the turmoil going on in front of his eyes. He somehow knew what he was watching did not concern him.

The now muddy street was filled with people rushing about heading toward where he knew the old mine entrance had been. Some of the people were carrying lanterns, others shovels

22

and picks. He heard muffled voices, as if coming from a long distance through a tunnel.

He watched the crowd draw aside for a man driving a horse-drawn buggy headed up the road in the opposite direction from the rest. Toward the center of town the buggy raced. The driver was missing his hat, face white and strained. He urged his horse to a run. Sid watched him round the corner toward the bookstore and disappear.

The eerie light was fading now; the images were flicking out like distortion on a TV screen. Still, a strange shimmer remained, covering the mud splattered roadway, the trees, and bushes.

Sid stood frozen in disbelief. What was he experiencing? He actually pinched himself.

"Ouch! Sid you are an idiot."

He had lived here in Black Diamond all of his life. He knew the history of the mines from his father and grandfather. He knew of mine cave-ins and the panic, terror, fear and sorrow they brought to the people of that time. Just what had happened here, he didn't know.

Although dark clouds still filled the sky, the rain had almost stopped. Fog was starting to swirl about just above the ground.

Once again he heard hoofs beating hard on the road. Racing through the swirling mist the buggy came toward him a wraithlike continuation of the waking dream he had just experienced.

He thought he saw a woman beside the man. The woman was in an odd black hat. He noticed that her face as white as flour. Sid watched as the buggy moved past him close enough to see the tears glistening on the woman's cheeks. Close enough for him to hear her say, "Please God, not John!"

A dense gathering of mist and fog blurred his view just as he could swear he saw the buggy turn into the entrance of the cemetery to the west of his house.

Rain continued to pelt down on his old hat dripping on to his shoulders. Shaking himself, Sid stumbled into his house, up the stairs and climbed in beside Joan. Pulling the covers up tight over his head, closing his eyes he prayed to God to let it all be a dream.

Morning came with dazzling sunlight dancing through the window. He realized he had forgotten to close the blinds when he had finally come to bed last night. Sid rubbed his eyes sitting abruptly straight up. He could smell coffee. Joan must be awake. Surely, this morning was the same as always. Gathering his wits about him, he dressed and went downstairs to the kitchen.

"Joan, I think I'll walk up to the bakery for some sweet rolls to add to that coffee. If you don't mind, that is."

He smiled at his wife as he gave her a good morning hug.

"Oh, go ahead." Joan patted his shoulder. "Maybe it'll wake you up, you sleepyhead."

Sid walked out into the sunshine as he concentrated on the familiar world about him. It all looked the same to him. He must have been dreaming last night.

He saw mud on the pavement, but he guessed that was because it had rained so hard in the night.

Topping the hill he spotted Bob on the porch of the bookstore.

When Sid came closer he realized Bob was sweeping partially dried mud out his door and off the porch.

"Good morning Bob." Sid called. "You're busy this morning. Where in the world did all that mud come from?"

"Hi Sid, I really don't know. It was this way when I came in. It was a peculiar night last night. Guess I shouldn't be surprised. Why don't you come on in and have a cup of coffee with me?"

Sid followed Bob into the building stopping just inside the door. Although Bob had certainly swept the floor it was still obvious someone had walked on the floor with muddy shoes.

Sid asked, "did someone invade your bookstore last night."

"Come around here." Bob said, pointing to two mugs side by side on the counter. "See those. Last night I had a visitor. It was a fairly different one at that. You might say a lady in distress. I left her sleeping in the back when I went home. This morning she was gone. The only thing left to let me know she was really here is that coffee mug, the one with the chip. She dropped it last night. Here let me pour you a cup."

Sid looked at Bob. "Bob, I had a strange dream last night."

He hesitated then told Bob what he had experienced in the night.

Frowning, Bob then told Sid all about Mrs. Samuelson and her son John. As an afterthought he added how he had found the crumpled blanket on the couch in the back of the store. He hesitated, and then showed Sid the small bowl of pecans.

The two men looked at one another in amazement.

"Let's look up something about mine cave-ins and see when the last big one was," Bob said, setting down his mug and turning to a book he already had opened on the counter.

Sure enough, there had been a cave-in eighty years ago on the very same date as last night.

"Sid, I have an idea. Want to go along with it?", Bob asked.

"I will if I can." Sid replied. "I'd like an answer to this strangeness so I can sleep tonight."

The two men jumped into Bob's car and headed north to the Black Diamond cemetery. Walking carefully through the headstones, reading every name, side by side they came to two stones that were identical. One read:

John M. Samuelson, killed in a mine cave-in April 13, 1903.

The one alongside read: Etta May Samuelson, Mother of John, died April 13, 1903 of a broken heart.

They stood there transfixed.

"Sid." Bob finally found the words to say. "I won't mention this to anyone, if you promise to do the same."

"It's a deal." Sid heaved a sigh of release. "Guess no one would believe us anyway."

The two men returned to the bookstore. As Sid was leaving, Bob said, "Why don't you take some of these delicious Virginia pecans to Joan. They are really special." Sid said, "Thank you; Joan will enjoy these."

The two men went about the remainder of their day with something of wonder and mystery hidden in their memories.

What makes a woman beautiful?
Her soul in shining armour
waiting for the trust
of temptation to divert;
to turn the tide of battle
'gainst the invited hurt,
Her kind and gentle manner
saying right will always win;
the way her trusting heart invites you in.

She questions not your reason,
but delivers you her faith;
and so you venture not to
harm or lose that place
within her precious confidence
that somehow grants it grace
to you, and wipes always all trace of sin.
so worthy may you be, her
heart to enter in.

What makes a woman beautiful?
'Tis not the tone of skin,
the color of her hair,
her nails so smoothly polished,
the fine clothes she may wear.
It's all so many other things
she sends forth from within;
it's the way her trusting
heart invites you in!

© 2013, Diana Harbeck

rain pastiche

don't know why
there's no sun up in the sky

yet my hands yearn, fingers yearn
as fresh-as-spring plants yearn
to be new settlers

outside   rain
straight   in parallel lines
like a child's   drawing

spearmint, orange mint, chocolate mint
all wait   longing to join the others
                a company of herbs

the rain speaks in syllables
that can't be found in our language
and so do the crows
        loud on the high slim branches

can't stop that yearn all day
to walk in the sun once more
replant the yawning clay pot
so close to the lime green one

a pot that happily boasts *"Old Faithful"*-
a bountiful, blooming chive
perpetually defiant

all day
that orderly rain
like a fate
uninterrupted by late love

until   *until*
at last a break   as over-worked clouds
take a time out   I race for the gloves

for the potting soil   race
for the mints, the rosemary, the sage
and begin

jaunty herbs start to sink
into their soft new bed
helped by a happy trowel

in the silence I still listen for drops
a mere six plops   can ruin a coif
and would you believe
that just now

with only oregano and thyme left to go
they fall   not even slow
without mercy   bloated drops fall

I gather tools, gloves, me
gain shelter faster
than a fairytale finale

indoors, I at last surrender
to an evening of unceasing music

rain falls heavily from the eaves
like a song played over and over
I am not even tired
and want the notes of the rain
to play like panpipes in the hidden places
where I think my soul lives
want them to take watery root there

© May 2014, Phyllis Williams ---
A Cento

David A. Bell ------ "Stormy Weather"
Jane Hirshfield --- "Two Rains"
Patricia Fargnoli –
"From a Rented Cottage" by
   Winnisquam in Rain

The Nuts and Bolts of Poetrics

Freely or challenged,
poetry flows ever forward
like a river's waters
singing in its depths
of channeled reverie.

Thoughts grouped and tuned, stanza as lines, or knot,
enjambing the reader who punctuates the page
by commas and semi colons of breath periodically
held or dismissed as starts and stops of wind on would.

The tones and hues evoked
so oftened, otherwise emblazoned,
analogously, complementarily
stoke the flames fed by fonts.

Sounds and particles repeated
paint a pattern or compose
a landscape portrayed, personified,
relayed by taut heart strings
or by timpani beating out a melody

as alliteration swings
with syncopation tapping
out syl-lab-if-i-cation
until words rewind, and
rebound, words resound...

An orchestra of metaphor often sets
out to test a score of coiled metallic conduits
as it weaves thoughts into bands of brass
around a core of great hyperbole and greater crafted simile.

Rhythmed~Rhymed,
(or free versed)
at once repetitive,
at once remitted,
at once remembered
for complexity
until in its intricate simplicity ends
in the final metered moment
of a quiet coda.

© 2016, Wendy N. Bell

The Nuts and I

© July 24, 2016, By Marjorie Eldred

Nuts and I have been good friends for more years than I can tell. My body, however, can testify to the long relationship. I believe my friendship with Nuts began when I was diagnosed with diabetes. That meant I should leave any relationship I'd previously had with Sugar and its friends Cookie, Cake, Candy, and any others who ran with that crowd. I'd never spent a lot of time or money on that crowd, but suddenly they became supremely attractive. It had something to do with the idea of leaving them alone.

I was diagnosed during my first pregnancy. My child-bearing years were just ahead. I'd been married less than a year. I wanted to cook for my husband and children, and I wanted to eat with them. Baking with my children playing around my feet with the pots and pans from my cupboard brought some of my happiest moments. However, the products of my labors tempted me, and I did some yielding. I almost lost a child I carried because I couldn't stay away from those sweets. It was a learning experience.

When I learned what indulging did to my body and that of my child I began to think differently. I realized more clearly what my choices were. I could continue to flirt with disaster and indulge in whatever I wanted, resulting in hospital stays, nerve pain, and perhaps loss of eyesight or my legs, or I could modify my diet and live a healthy life in spite of my diabetes. I chose the latter.

That's when my friendship with Nuts developed. I began to dream of planting a pecan tree in my back yard. I found Nuts to be a friendly face in a world of Enemies. I read most Nuts are full of the healthy omega-three oils which are the healthy fats everyone needs in their diets. Nuts don't add Sugar to your diet. They provide a great way to snack and keep blood glucose in control as well. The problem I had with Nuts, however, was I couldn't stop with one handful but kept returning for another. I've never had a problem with gaining weight, but Nuts soon showed me he could add pounds pretty well, and loved to do it for me.

When I went for my check-ups and found I'd put on several pounds I stayed away from the Nut gang until I lost the extra weight, but I could never break the relationship with those Nuts. Now that I'm older I find it a bit more difficult to keep the results of my fellowship with Nuts off my tummy and hips. Will I change my crowd and resort to the Vegetable gang for friends? They'd never fill the empty space in my tummy as well or keep me so happy. Nut gang, here I come.

Reflected Consideration

Her smile
When prescription
Matches fantasy

© 7-29-2016, K. S. Lapham

It May Be English but it's Different Here
© 26 March 2010, R. S. Gaylord

It's hard enough to adjust to the time change in Australia but I had to re-learn to drive. The Aussies copied the British, I guess, and they all drive on the wrong side of the street, or so it would seem to an American.

It feels strange to sit on the right side of the car to steer. Even more difficult for me, was the fact the dang little cars' controls are changed too. The "job assignments" are reversed so my left hand seemed to be happy it had more to do. But my right hand was frustrated by the opposite control responsibilities for shifting, windshield wiper control and using the turn indicators. There even seemed to be a subtle battle between the left and right sides of my body; *hey, who's in charge here?*

The first afternoon, I wanted to get something at a nearby store. When I turned to leave the parking lot I repeated the usual, *sitting-on-the-right-side-of-an-automobile,* American driver's confusion again and accidently flipped on the windshield wipers instead of the turn indicator.

I had already been told most newly arriving drivers, learning for the first time about driving from the right side of the car, will invariably engage the lever that turns on the windshield wipers instead of properly signaling a turn. I was warned that the police will stop a person for failure to properly signal a turn when they see that happen.

I goofed. Sure enough, I was immediately stopped by the police. I pulled over to the left curb, rolled down my window and waited.

"You failed to signal your turn leaving the parking lot," the officer said as she came up to my window.

I acknowledged the failure and explained, "I just arrived today and haven't had time to get completely used to the different driving situation here in Australia."

She smiled and asked to see my license.

I extracted my California Drivers' License and handed it out

34

to her.

She looked then frowned and asked, "Where is your International Drivers' License?"

"I don't have an International License."

She then raised her voice somewhat, speaking slowly, "You must have an International License when you come from a foreign country to Australia and expect to drive here."

I was puzzled by this statement, "I asked the people at Hertz and they said I didn't need an International License."

"Who?"

"Hertz," I answered.

"What?" she asked, leaning forward almost into the window of my rental car.

"Hertz" I answered again.

"What hurts?" She asked me.

Getting frustrated, I raised my voice and repeated, "Hertz, Hertz, you know, the people where I rented the car." The officer stepped back staring at me.

Her partner walked up showing a broad smile. She turned in frustration to him. He then said with confidence, what sounded to me like, "I believe it's a cawfohire."

The first officer turned to me and said, "Oh, cawfohire, is that right?"

"What?" I asked.

They said in unison, "Cawfohire."

I sat in a dull silence then realized they both had said, "Car for hire."

I said, "Oh, yes, it's a car for hire, we call that a rental car. The company I rented from is Hertz. The folks at the desk said it's OK to drive without an International License."

"Very well sir, please drive carefully while you develop the skill needed to drive here," the male officer said and they both returned to the patrol car shaking their heads.

Then, oddly, I spoke at my hands on the wheel and said, "Would you two guys get it sorted out? We were almost busted."

35

The Nuts and Bolts of My Dad

My dad is a good man,
An old man now.
When young, he did seed, chop and plow,
Now elderly, widowed, but clings to his marital vow.

In high school he was bullied–
Dropped out to escape the torment.
He worked hard to satisfy every need,
Always watched every single cent.

He and his twin purchased a red combine;
They went south and north to harvest wheat.
His God-fearing morals forever genuine,
He fought hard against defeat.

In the fifties, he was an Army captain.
Deuce & a half trucks he drove o'er the Golden Gate.
As he ages he recounts his days in the Pacific sun
But his heart is broken for his lost mate.

Fathered seven children, buried one baby.
This quiet man never raised his voice
But honored his young wife as a lady.
Loving her was his privilege, his choice.

He sold the farm in favor of the lumber trade
And built a new house with his bare hands.
From acorns he's grown many oaks for shade
And whistle the tunes of good old country bands.

In his gray-haired years he slowed down;
He and his twin turned 80 and earned a large party—
The event drew a large crowd in their hometown.
Laughter, food, and family—all fun and hearty.

When his wife succumbed to cancer
He refused to dispose of her things.
For over sixty years his focus has been on her--
With his love he gave her the nuts and bolts
To live forever with angel wings.

© 2016, by Marilyn White

The Nut and the Beauty Salon

Tiffany started out the door,
"Going to town to do some chores.
Hair needs cut, nails need done."
When Johnny heard, he wanted fun.
"I'm goin' along" he told his girl.
"Maybe I'll get my hair a curl."

He followed her to the nail salon.
When it came to color, "What do you think, Hon?
I'm goin' to get me a pedicure.
If you ask me why, I'm not real sure.
Togetherness is a real good plan,
So why is color banned for man?"

When choosing color, he picked up green,
then the wildest assortment you've ever seen,
Red and purple and yellow and pink,
"One color each toe, I really think,"
He told his attendant, and at her scowl
our Johnny hid behind the towel.

The 'beauty' plan completed now
He preened for Tiff and took a bow.
But don't you know as time wore on
Began to wish the colors gone.

Decided one day to take a skate
So got his board, just couldn't wait.
He had such fun until he flipped
And came back down with his 'wings clipped'
A broken leg he had to show.
Medics, hospital, don't you know?

They'll take off my shoe! Our Johnny thought.
They'll see the polish, I'll get caught!"
And caught he was. They thought it funny.
Paraded him 'round upon the gurney
And told him, up and down the hall,
To show his 'rainbow toes' to all.

Our Johnny felt like such a dolt
If he had a choice he'd choose to bolt
But trapped he was upon the gurney
Believe me folks, that wasn't funny!
So there he stayed while people laughed
And heard them say," That fellow's daft"

He learned a lesson well that day:
Be careful when you go to play.
And make your choices carefully.
Cause what you do they'll surely see.
Don't follow your girl to the beauty salon.
With rainbow toes your dignity's gone.

© 2010, Marjorie Eldred

The Industry Of Making; Making It Through Life.

All night the great wheel turns. Every night
it turns and churns and creaks and lets out hisses
relentless through every hour, minute after minute
never missing any second of the weeks and months
and years driving ever forward through each motion,
each rotation, every circulation of its size, each circumference
calculated three point one four one five, four times "r" the radius,
that point from the center measured to the outer rim,
that edge honed and hardened by the effort working
its way ahead as the years pile on the distance measuring,
every strive adding up the feet into the miles and miles
of circumnavigation counting up the days. It moans
and groans and works its way in the heat and fire,
the noise and hot commotion of machinery through
every day and keeps the vigil up throughout the night
without fail until suddenly, as if there was to be no tomorrow
it stops still. There is no forewarning, no bells or whistles
to indicate a breakdown, no added creaks or grinding gears,
abbot, no retirement celebration. It just sticks still
in place and will not budge. The world grows cold,
turns sharp and dark and dims under a dengue of deep gray boiling
pressing down on the process, draining out the energy of life's work
let go. All is grounded to a halt as all its effort, all the trying,
all the forward notions slip behind. The great wheel is dead still
as it is released, as it relieves the great strain of pulling life's weight
up and up the hill, no stop, no plateau to wait and rest upon attempting
to achieve the crown. It simply sighs a great relief and dies.

© 2016, Alan C. Keimig

The Machinery Turn Into Life

Every day the nuts and bolts, taut and tightened
keep operational, well-oiled, a lubricated, finely tuned
congress of a well-managed affair, precisely maintained
that tics and tocks its way ahead counting out
the minutes into hours and hours like clockwork
through the days on into the night until all the rest
is its history, one set common to its cause, purposeful,
one set of circumstance that work and work one way
even as it added on new ways, methods made to do for it
and it alone as it labors on, not apart, but certainly
separate, alongside all that was and all that comes into contact
with the working of the parts as they churn and turn
it into progress with each measured goal tied to
the clank and clanging mechanism in the harmonics
of the harmony tuned so all the effort gains solid footing.
It is each machine in the machinery of the whole,
one within the other humming in unison, with unity,
working for the benefit of each to secure a solid place
to steady up the climb. And while some take the harder course
many choose the routes less sheer, with less strain,
less wear and tear, no matter, eventually all break down,
little by little, parts become undone, the pieces begin to fray,
fall in disrepair. Though functioning for awhile at half speed,
the days start numbering. And though just slow
the work declines steadily, grinding to a halt,
the purpose, so long well serving now needs served.
All the energy well placed, once a certainty is not
while the appreciation of their effort is admired
in the end all is wished well, thanks given for the industry
so long, so well applied and now it's stopped, locked into eternity.
The silent machinery turned to deafening that it no longer operates.

© 2016, Alan C. Keimig

Critic's Corner
© 2006, Paul T. Jackson

Why, just the other day I did a dumb thing. And most of the time I look at all the dumb things I do and often wonder why this happens; was it intentional? What was the motivation to do these dumb things anyway? Is it time to write about the critics in all of us?

We listen to the music and movie critics as if they are not flawed persons and can tell us exactly all the time, what we need to know. But do we often find the critics are wrong? Of course we do. Does that mean my dumb things might be smart things?

What about those Dummies books? I've written about this before. It seems that we are all dummies and even proclaim to be when we buy these books. How can we all be so dumb? Actually the Dummies and Complete Idiot books were supposed to make things easier for us dummies. Did they? Not the ones I bought! They told me to do things that didn't work; try things I couldn't try because by the time the book was available things had already changed to something else. I was a critic of the book, "Leadership for Dummies." Who would want to be lead by someone who though he/she was a dummy leader?

We criticize ourselves so much; we have fun putting down others for whatever reason. That's why Celebrity Roasts are so popular, I suppose. Why if we didn't have others, as well as ourselves to criticize, what would we honestly joke and talk about? I guess the weather; but don't we criticize that also? It's too hot. It's too cold. It's too windy. It's too much the same day in and day out; boy am I tired of this. Of course, it's too muggy. Now there's a word, Muggy. It's supposedly a descriptive word, but when we use it, are we not criticizing the weather? I wonder what they call words that criticize as well as describe – pejorative?

I know a few people who would have a lot to talk about all the time and not at all be self-critical. In fact they are so overwhelmingly interested in themselves they don't know when to shut up. They remind me of Emily Dickerson's poem, "I'm nobody, who are you?" Except they are the reverse. I'm somebody; do I know you? And, "It's nice seeing me!" But alas, I criticize again.

Again and again we seem to be looking for something we don't like and attack it with all our souls -- including ourselves. Take driving, for instance. Is there anyone who doesn't at least think critically about the driver who pulls in front of you, then slows down to give himself room between him/her and the car in front of him/her, leaving you with virtually none between you and the interloper? But when we do the same things, do we criticize ourselves?

We are told we are created in God's image, a gift of God? Or is that something to critique. Why, God, did you give me red hair? Why, God, did you give me a long nose, neck, arms, or skinny legs? Why, God, did you give me this life, when you knew it would be a struggle for me? Why can't I have more fun, God? I just want to have fun. These are all critiques about ourselves basically, not God.

I'm wondering if we were not able to critique anyone; the football team, its coach, the players individually, or our church members—you know the ones that wear too much makeup or the dowdy person who always sits where you want to sit. What would we do then? What about that kitchen? It needs to be remodeled. Our house needs to expand. Our house needs to be rebuilt. I need a house. There's a topic for another article.

It would seem that we are, on the one hand, destined to be upset. Are we unwilling to find good things, or are we the optimists always looking for something better, something more outstanding, something that will, in fact, make both our lives and others, something to be enjoyed, or make it better for others in the future?

The perspective is perhaps critics are those who seek a better world for all of us—including ourselves. And how can that be bad?

I recently complained that the band T-shirts, the color of grey heather, weren't very snazzy and reminded me of getting ready to go to the gym, rather than a razzle, dazzle, give-the-audience-a-fun time concert. I suspect, for some, going to the gym is like getting ready for church, so why do I criticize? It must be me again, always about me and how I feel, and the expectations I have of others.

I'm glad we ask questions that help us make things better, whether it's about new products that make things easier, or save us time or money, or make us safer. Whether these questions are critiques or complaints, they do have a wonderful way to get people thinking about what they are doing, how they are doing it, whether it can be done differently for a better result, whether there is any reason to do what we are doing the same way or not.

In some ways the consultant is hired to ask dumb questions, not because we feel we may be doing dumb things, but because we want an outside look at what is being done and if there is a way to improve.

So we come back to the critic. Are we destined to *improve* because we criticize or are we criticizing always in order to prove to others we know best and are doing what we do better than the other person? I'm thinking the act of criticizing may be the *nuts and bolts* which bind us together for better lives. Everyone has a different perspective and if we listen to the critics, perhaps we will come together as a community to solve problems positively.

Working To Preserve

The rusty bolt refused to turn, the nut holding
firmly from the years left open to the elements,
which welded it with wind and rain, freezing cold,
with ice and snow, then summer heat that forged
them both into one association that will not budge.
Iron is obstinate this way, strong, resistant to the will
much like the old people from these parts hanging on,
those who first came here and cranked these both
together tight to hold the structure rigid through the time,
just like their resolve to build the solid foundation
of their lives firmly pinned to the land they settled in,
self reliant, doing everything the first time right,
so it didn't have to be redone, the days too few
to redo with all that needed to be achieved
to make the wilderness a home, struggling too
as I struggle now with their work on this bolt
and nut trying to save a lasting posterity
in these valued pieces from their lives to carry on
with mine, with reverence for the traditions
that brought them all this far with relevance, with resiliency
and self respect. This is the bolts and nuts I have
learning now how to become myself like them.

© 2016, Alan C. Keimig

TEXAS EDUCATION: THE KING RANCH
© January 2015, R. S. Gaylord

    Many years ago, my wife and I were visiting our daughter in Port Isabel, Texas, when we read in the local newspaper about an educational trip nearby. We both agreed we could learn more about Texas by signing up for that particular educational trip. A good feature we recognized was all the traveling for this would take place in just one day while our daughter would be at work. The news article said it was a very interesting Texas history lesson which included some bird watching and animal viewing. Most of it would be primarily focused on the King Ranch. We had already heard this ranch was an important cultural contribution to Texas history. We decided to learn more and signed up.

    A small bus picked us up at 7:10 a.m., stopped a few times to pick up others and then shuttled us off to near-by Harlingen, Texas, where we pulled into a large hotel's parking lot. There, we boarded a much bigger bus, filled with folks who were also eager to learn more about Texas. Right away we discovered our larger bus had a woman on board as our teacher. Soon we headed off down US 77; we were told we were going to Kingsville, Texas. As we travelled past Raymondville, we were informed by our teacher, "Most of the way we are going now is still, or was once, the King Ranch."

    Hearing this, my wife and I smiled at each other. I said, "I'll bet the city of Kingsville is not only named after the ranch it may even be on ranch property."

    Our teacher gestured out the side window and told us there is still some of the Yturria family's ranch along the way here. She said the owners are still Mexican citizens. Then she explained, "However, from now on, most of our hour-and-a-half drive, at 60 mph, will be along the King Ranch property line."

    Everyone on our bus seemed to be amazed by what she told us about the size of this privately-owned property. She then said, "It was 1.2 million acres at one time, but their children have been spinning off some and the Texas Kenedy family broke off long ago from being a partner, so now the ranch is only 825 thousand acres." She then smiled and said, "However, it is still as large as the state of Rhode Island."

Next she passed around a map of the area and said, "It continues to be wholly owned by one family of the King's descendants, the family name now is Kleberg."

When we saw the map of the ranch area it appeared to be so amazingly huge it was hard for us to grasp. The map seemed to show it in four huge pieces of land that didn't touch anymore. We wondered if maybe the separation happened when the Kenedy family was given some of the original ranch property.

She went on to explain more about the ranch history. Over time, when a family member decided to sell their shares, some other family member would buy them out. However, many years ago after two King daughters sold out, a son asked for a spin-off of 40 thousand acres to farm; he did not intend to raise cattle. Finally one daughter married a lawyer who wanted to be a cowboy, his name was Kleberg. Their descendants now run the ranch. All the Klebergs are cowboys or cowgirls and they seem to love it. The ranch itself is no longer in the hands of any family members with the name King.

The teacher went on to say she thought it was possible King may not have been the original owner's real name, because he was Irish. She then informed us he ran off as an unwanted small boy and made his own way in life. He may have changed his name as he got rich by trading in cotton. Then he bought up the Mexican grants of land all over this part of the state of Texas. He died young and his wife ran the ranch for forty years after his death. They had five children. The oldest son who loved being a cowboy died and, with time, the others gave up and left, except for the one daughter, Mrs. Kleberg. The Kleberg family dominates the area now, owning many things like banks and retail stores in Kingsville, Texas, a nearby town.

As we were absorbing the teacher's discussion of the history of the ranch, our bus entered the town of Kingsville where we would continue our education. As we looked around my wife noted, "Sure enough, a large number of facilities in town are indeed owned by the Kleberg family, you can see their name on them."

We parked and everyone got out of the bus. We were on our own for a while to enjoy the town. At one Kleberg retail store, named *The Kleberg Saddle Shop*, my wife bought a lovely purse. What a magnificent, up-scale store it was too. We both enjoyed visiting the store and the town of Kingsville as part of our educational program.

Our group discussed the interesting education to this point, as we all gathered once again; this time to enjoy lunch together in Kingsville.

After lunch we boarded the bus and drove onto the actual ranch property. As our bus slowly proceeded along one of the ranch roads, our teacher pointed out through a window, telling us, "Please look over here, close to this side of the bus are two new breeds of cattle. They were developed on the King Ranch."

We could see a large number of cattle scattered across the landscape. The distinctly different breeds developed by the ranch were interesting to observe.

She told us the ranch also takes credit for the quarter horse, which she said was apparently first developed on this ranch.

The highlight of the trip for us occurred when we saw a wild pig that was obviously in love with one of the ranch cattle, which was a bull! The wild pig ignored the bus and pursued its chosen bull with a passion. Our guide, who we learned was a crusty old cowgirl herself, said on all her teaching and wrangling trips she had never seen one of these wild pigs, even though many live on the King Ranch. She said it was because they are so easily spooked. The bus load of people laughed and laughed to watch the persistence of this little pig chasing the big bull in the nearby pasture. The bull kept moving away as the little pig maintained hot pursuit.

We ended our ranch visit with a real Texas BBQ at one of the

48

old bunk houses. Some added learning occurred there, in the building, as we were shown a picture of hunters who were hanging on the outside of an interesting elongated automobile. She explained many folks pay to hunt deer on this ranch every year.

The teacher went through lots of history of the origin of the King Ranch and their branding symbol which looks something like a smoothly written W while the Bar-B-Q was cooking over an open fire. When it was time to serve the dinner we all sat outside around the fireplace to consume our choice of brisket, sausage, pickles, onions, jalapenos, thick slices of white bread, and coleslaw. All guests finished the evening with a marshmallow roast over the open fire.

Now we know more about Texas.

Who We Do Become

Weather borne, beaten back,
well leathered in the heat
and cold, dry wind, winter's
frost and summer's indifferent
sun that moulds into the
surviving years the character
that grows beneath the skin
in spirit, mind, and body
broken, bent, that is this beauty
aged to perfection in complexities
and high in every avenue across
the land and ocean's equal face.
It is the life that settles in its place
that makes us who we do become.

© 2006 Alan C Keimig

The Build Up of the Cheeseburger

Oh juicy, hot, delectable combination
Cheeseburgers are treasures of our American nation,
In the simplest well-established form:
A patty, cheese, and two buns served toasty warm.

The word itself is a portmanteau
A double is enhanced with meat times two.
Plain or with toppings, all can agree
A triple cheeseburger is patty times three.

Certainly alternative varieties of cheese
Sophisticate up this simple entree', oh please!
Brie, stilton, pepper jack, Asiago or feta,
Sharp cheddar, Swiss, bleu cheese, or Velveeta.

Kick it up a notch, not only ketchup and mustard;
Add mayo with guacamole and fresh garlic custard.
Smear on almond butter to the hot beefy surface;
And wipe off that 1000-Island from your face.

Now consider the onions: raw or grilled?
Add pickles, tomato, and olives pimento filled;
How about kale, crimini mushrooms, or sauerkraut?
Red peppers, cashews, or bacon need not be left out.

More odd enhancements to the basic cheeseburger
Are anchovies, horseradish, and jalapenos for fire;
A fried egg, pat of butter, slice of ham, or bits of tofu.
Mull over salsa or chili to spice up this burger for you.

The cheeseburger's beginning in history
Remains somewhat of a mystery.
More than one individual lay competing claim–
Of cheeseburger's first invention they all proclaim.

O'Dell's Restaurant in LA sold for twenty-five cents
A chili cheeseburger in '28 they certainly argue.
Two years later, Steak n' Shake's Gus Belt

Trademarked his own burger with cheese melt.

Consider Kaeilin's of Louisville in 1934
Who served cheeseburgers—so is the folklore.
The next year in Denver, Humpty Dumpty's did win
The trademark award at their little drive-in.

In 1956 a small Kansas café called "The What Spot"
Calls dibs on the cheeseburger's #1 discovery slot
When little Tanya Stern sliced American cheese
And added it to her sizzling beef patty, aha cheez whiz!

The cheeseburger is not kosher in Israel,
A New York City variation is quite controversial;
Their cheese of choice is that made of soy,
Now Jews in Brooklyn may feel free to devour, oh joy!

A song called *Cheeseburger in Paradise* by Jimmy Buffett
Exclaims in his lyrics: in his daydreams this sensuous treat,
"Medium rare with Muenster'd by nice," (you can't beat)
"A big warm bun and a huge hunk of meat."

Yes, everyone knows that burgers and fries
Are not for weight-loss, but are indeed paradise!
Cheeseburgers certainly have too many calories-
Upwards of 600 and can nearly triple that, oh geez!

Stick with my diet, I chant and lament
No cheeseburgers tonight, alas it's torment.
For dinner: no single, no double, not even a half-patty,
Only lettuce, tomato, and pickles for miserable me.

Mr. Cheeseburger, for you there's one day set aside
As the American Day to celebrate nationwide.
September 18 is the holiday to let your teeth sink in
It's a party, a win-win, and that day ain't no sin.
It's National Cheeseburger Day! Hip Hip Hooray!

© 2013, Marilyn White

"Sort Of, Will Never Do"
© 2016, by JoAnn Jackson

The weather-beaten face of the white-haired old man was bent over a work bench, deep in concentration. His eyes were focused on an old blue bicycle. He was not alone in the workshop, but might as well have been. His grandson, Randy, sitting nearby knew his job was to watch without interruption.

Opa, as he was known to the boy, walked over to look at a wall of interesting old drawers. His hand went to his chin. Scratching his unshaven face, he studied the wall of shiny metal bins.

The small boy could not stand the quiet any longer. "Opa, what are you looking for?"

"A bolt, but it has to be just the right size. And it has to have the correct head on it.

Sort of, will never do," Opa replied as he smiled at Randy.

His grandson watched as Opa finally chose a drawer to pull out and carefully inspect. While he was looking in the drawer, he pushed his rimless glasses up on the top of his head.

I would think he would need his glasses to look at those things in the drawer, the boy observed.

After having taken down several different drawers, pushing the contents around, and then putting the drawers back, Opa looked up, smiling at his grandson. This was the bolt he had been looking for. It was short, thick and had a flat head on it so when screwed in it would be even with the surface. The other end would have a round nut put on it.

"Always take the time to find the right one, Randy. Sort of will never do," Opa said quietly to his grandson. Then Opa motioned for the boy to come closer. The old man put his well-worn screwdriver in the boy's hand. "I'll hold the nut in place while you screw it on, boy."

Randy moved next to his grandfather with a sense of pride. He was now old enough to participate in the repair of something,

52

not just an observer. He took the handle of the screwdriver in his own small hand. Randy felt its warmness left from Opa's hand. He ran a finger over the handle feeling how smooth the ridges were.

This seemed to be the beginning of Randy's life. He now wanted to fix things. He wanted to make things better. He wanted to create things.

"When can we go to Opa's?" was a frequent plea from Randy. In the past, the grandfather had usually not been a focus. He was usually out in his workshop, while Oma (grandmother) had been more of an interest as she was the source of cookies freely given in between hugs.

I love the smells in Oma's house. It always smells like honey and cinnamon. Randy thought about ways to spend more time there. His parents both worked now that he had started school.

School. School. Hmmm. Summer is almost over. I think it is bad for me to repeat Kindergarten. I am so tall, and all my friends are going to be in first grade. I guess I should have wanted to be a good student. But…It wasn't any fun.

When school started, he was not especially eager to go. This year, Randy had a new teacher, Mrs. Fleming. She made school interesting. Being the "older" guy in class, he knew the ropes.

Mrs. Fleming saw new maturity in the boy. His last teacher had talked about Randy to her and why she thought he should stay back. He had not shown an ability to recognize all the letters or write them. He counted to 20 but never seemed to go further. He had no focus in class and did not interact much with others.

What Mrs. Fleming now saw was a boy who wanted to know everything, asked many questions. He suddenly showed that indeed he knew his letters and their sounds and knew some words, he just did not want to go through regimen. He seemed apart from the class. During playtime he sought out blocks and things he could manipulate.

"Your son's structures in the block area are very complex," his parents were told during the first conference. "He does know his letters, sounds, and will count forever if I let him. His printing is improving. He is polite to others but does not really interact. When left to himself, he looks at books. I haven't tested his reading ability yet, but I am aware he knows and reads many subjects." This was the report from this new teacher.

Randy's parents were relieved he was showing ability, but were baffled it had not been apparent last year. They looked at each other. Had they made a mistake in keeping him in the same grade a second year?

It was decided since his birthday was a summer one, he should stay where he was and be the big fish in the pond. Mrs. Fleming assured them she would find ways to challenge him.

Randy's life had improved immensely; he had a teacher he admired and who would challenge him. The kids in class were okay, but he only developed one close friendship. But Timmy was all he needed it seemed. Then a new ray of sunshine came into his life. Opa was elected to pick him up every day after school.

They would often go for rides in his big red car during which Opa would tell him stories, both real and imaginative. A snack would be waiting for him when they got home. Oma would have fruit waiting for him and his favorite, 'nuts and bolts' was always at hand. *How did she make that?* Randy wondered. He had never seen her do it.

Mrs. Fleming developed a new program just for Randy. He was given special instruction each day by Mrs. Albert, who came into class one hour each day. She spent time on a computer with Randy; he was given special books to read. He did this while everyone else was learning their letters. Mrs. Fleming gave him "homework" every day---which was the work everyone else did in class that day. Randy had not yet learned to write his letters properly, so he did that with the class. Play time was almost always he and Timmy building some special structure. Mrs. Fleming soon learned to tell them to pick up before the others as it took them so long to put all the blocks away in their proper places.

Opa and Randy went for walks together as well as rides in that wonderful red car. Part of the day was always spent in the workshop, where Randy learned more about tools, how to use them, and how to make things.

Randy took a serious interest in reading, something he had not been too excited about before. But if the book or magazine talked about repair or design, he couldn't wait to open it.

At the end of the school year it was decided he would not need first grade, but should go to second grade and be with his peers. Randy could not wait for school to start this year. He had learned what school had to offer.

The summer after second grade, Randy took on odd jobs from neighbors. He asked to mow lawns, carried in groceries, washed cars, anything to earn money. He started going to the library to find books and magazines about repair and mechanical things.

The library was only a few blocks away from his grandparents' house so when he was in third grade, they started letting him go on his own. At first his mother objected to his riding his bicycle there, but he finally convinced her that eight was old enough to do this on his own.

Randy asked for a space of his own in the garage. He made a shelf to put jars he had collected from his mother and neighbors. Then he began to buy things he needed. He went to nearby garage sales. The boy found he could buy tools there he could not afford to buy at a store.

Soon Randy was repairing his own bicycle and began offering to fix his friends' bikes as well. His general attitude was happy. His life was good.

The next few years went by very quickly, he was restless at school as he always seemed to want to know more. He was lucky, as most of his teachers recognized these special talents of his and some developed special programs in class for him. All through his school years Timmy remained his friend, but he was now called Tim. Even though Tim was younger, he grew to be much taller than Randy. He felt his future lay in basketball. He had a hoop at his house where he and Randy spent their time shooting baskets together when not in Randy's workshop.

The boy read a book about an unusual bicycle. It was made in 1896. It was called the Horizontal Bicycelle Normal. This was a bicycle Randy had never seen. He had never heard the word recumbent. He began to look for books which had pictures of other recumbents as well as other oddly designed bicycles.

Randy had an idea about making a different kind of bicycle. He began collecting parts of bicycles from anywhere he could find them. His parents began to complain about the pile of scrap metal he was acquiring. The boy also saw that he did not have a good way to keep all of his collection dry.

Randy thought about one of their neighbors. Mrs. Weatherby, who lived down the street was in her 70's and did not have a car. But she did have a garage. It was full of discarded things collected and then forgotten.

One day Randy went to Mrs. Weatherby's door and rang the bell.

"Mrs. Weatherby." He paused before continuing. Then, getting up his nerve, "I was noticing the other day you have a lot of stuff in your garage," Randy looked up at her, not quite sure how to bring up what he had in mind.

Mrs. Weatherby smiled and said, "Yes, Randy, far too many things. I've collected things and now I don't know what to do with them all."

Offering her his brightest smile, he said, "I have an idea; I think it would help both of us." Taking a big breath, he went on. I would be happy to clean it out with you deciding what to do with things—if I could use a part of it for a workshop." Hurriedly he added, "I would pay you to use it. It wouldn't be much, but I am pretty good at earning money."

"Hmmm. An interesting idea," the old lady said. "Let me think about it. Come back tomorrow."

Randy shook his head affirmatively and said, "I'll be here at noon, ma'am."

Mrs. Weatherby and Randy came to an agreement the next day. Randy asked her how soon he could start. He agreed to come at 9:00 the next morning.

The two of them faced the contents of the garage at exactly 9:00. Randy had made sure he was on time so she would not change her mind.

The day started in cool weather but soon grew hot. The temperature was soon in the 90's, but Randy was a determined twelve-year-old. He was perspiring heavily as he sorted and got things ready for the junk man to come. Mrs. Weatherby came out from time to time to see what he had found. A few things she reclaimed and took into the house; others she called her daughter to see if she wanted.

Mrs. Weatherby's deceased husband had left a number of tools. Mrs. Weatherby's daughter was not interested in them. Mrs. Weatherby and Randy decided they should remain in the garage for Randy's use.

"Randy, would you like a glass of ice-cold lemonade?" He wiped his forehead with his arm, thanked her, and joined her on the back porch where the frosty lemonade glass was sitting. Next to it was a plate of freshly baked sugar cookies. The sugar was sparkling in the sunshine as if beckoning him. His stomach growled with anticipation.

"Thank you ma'am," Randy said politely. He sat down on the weather-beaten top step of the porch to savor each bite; then washed it down with the ice-cold lemonade. He drank too much at once, giving him a cold headache. He would have to sit a few minutes before having more.

Randy heard music coming from inside the house, a kind of music he had not heard before. He realized he could not understand the words, but he loved the melodies he was hearing. He asked Mrs. Weatherby about it. She told him it was music called opera. It was coming from a place in New York City. It was broadcast every Saturday, featuring a different opera each time.

Randy wanted to hear more.

When Randy was finished sorting everything in the garage, the Salvation Army was called to come collect what they deemed useful. Everything else was sitting there waiting for the junk man. When he came he noted there were no metal pieces, yet there were some in the garage. Randy quickly informed him that he had uses for many of them.

Opa had heard of Randy's new venture. His eyes grew watery thinking about what he may have started. Randy had several conversations with his parents at the beginning of the next school year. He finally had his way, he was now old enough to go to Oma and Opa's to do his homework, have a snack, then Opa would take him home where he would change and be allowed to go to his workshop. Opa would come from time to time to see what Randy was making, offering suggestions or information on how to use a tool. Opa had to be present if he was using anything motorized such as a saw or drill press. Oma always had a small bag of his favorite snack of 'nuts and bolts' to go with him.

One day Oma showed him how to make his favorite snack, the 'nuts and bolts' so he could start making his own. He made a list to go to the store with: Chex Mix, pretzels, (he preferred the round ones), Cheerios, nuts (pecans were best he thought), raisins, with a few chocolate chips thrown in. He also needed a little butter and a clove of garlic. He would ask his mother for—*sort of, would never do.*

"Thank you Oma," Randy said as he hugged her after they looked at this fresh supply of what he loved to nibble on.

Birthdays and Christmas' came with lists beforehand of things he needed for his workshop of special projects. Saturday mornings he could always be counted on to be in his workshop, listening to the Met while he worked. There was always a jar of 'nuts and bolts' sitting within reach.

School went quickly each year as he grew; everything seemed easier the older he got. Others did not really know what to make of him but he was always cheerful and willing to help others. At

Christmas his favorite thing to do was deliver bicycles he had fixed and painted to children who he knew could not afford one. He made a special four- wheeled bike for a boy who could not walk as his balance was too poor.

Randy's world revolved around a very strange collection of things. Then in his junior year a man came to school to interview him. The man asked to meet with his parents.

He had not identified himself, only that he wanted an interview with Randy's parents.

"We have been told about your son and his exceptional abilities. We have looked at his records, spoken with his teachers, and talked with him. We feel he is the kind of young man we would love have attend our school." With that he reached into his breast pocket, opened a small billfold with cards in it and handed one to the speechless parents. It identified him as someone representing Massachusetts Institute of Technology.

"MIT?" Randy's father exclaimed.

Randy's mother and father stared at each other.

"We are flattered," said his mother, but there is no way we can afford for him to go to such a school."

The man stared at them, then the table. Tapped his index finger on the table, and then looked up at them. He smiled. "I am offering him a free ride, everything. Can you afford the plane ride there? If not, we can probably provide it."

Randy's parents were stunned; speechless.

"We all need to talk. This is so---unexpected," Randy's father said.

"I'll be back on Friday, to answer any questions. I'll have papers for you as well. We want your young man, we don't want him to shine at some other school."

"Oh, by the way, we would like him to attend a special class at the University of Washington this summer—at our expense of course. Would that be possible?"

Randy and his family had a big conference to discuss possibilities. It became clear they needed more time to consider this.

"This has to be thought over carefully," Opa said.

Randy spoke up, "Yes, only the right place, the wrong choice will never do."

A decision was made, the time flew by and it was time for Randy to enter college. Opa stood at the airport trying to hold back tears of joy as he gripped his grandson around the shoulders before Randy launched into a whole new world. His whole family and Tim were there, seeing him off at the airport to his new life at MIT. In his bag was something special from Oma—a bag of 'nuts and bolts'.

Long Lake - July

Calm on the lake
day after the 4th
sun on leaves
squirrel on feeder
chippy on ground

no sounds
but bird twitters
and tweets
healing happening
peace prevails

© 2016, Isabel Jackson

60

A Personal Obituary

The time came when I,
Though through life's riches tread,
Upon a bed of needles and pine,
I went to lay my head.

Life, with all its sweet sublime ideals,
Which now is foiled like thistledown,
Errant from the calling of the land,
Life, the trickster, the rascal, the clown.

Though I was a happy being,
'Twas a trivial life I knew,
Only one in a vast empire,
Till at last the fatal rendezvous.

Every little mistake I made,
Looking back I see,
I paid no heed to the proverb,
"The best things in life are free."

© 2016 Jeanette Hallock

Memoir Baking
A Nearly Lost Chapter from Our Time in the Second Burien House: December 1954.
© 2016, Phyllis Bjork Williams

Most of my gardening time happened when sons Dan, four, and Tom, two, took two-hour afternoon naps. But by December, not much gardening happened. Instead, one day while they slept, I took out the Christmas cookie cutters that Florence Bjork, my cousin-in-law, had given me. She was "*Competence Personified,*" a very experienced and knowledgeable RN, a wonderfully involved mother of three teenagers, loving wife, and hostess to the Western world. At holiday time she made several hundred, lovely to look at, delightful to savor, cookies.

Once I opened the box of cutters and read pages of the directions, I knew the task would be daunting. Not only would I need to make just the right dough, but getting the red plastic replicas of Santa, Christmas tree, stocking, star and snowman to release that dough onto the baking sheets could be even trickier. *It turned out to be crazy-making.* Then, once the cookies were in and out of the oven, they not only would need icing and red or green sprinkles to cover areas like Santa's coat or the tree's branches, but a paint brush with delicate colors to complete subtle areas like Santa's cheeks and nose. Even though by then I'd been a homemaker for five years, I still felt nervous and a novice at many culinary tasks.

During all of my growing up years my stepmother did not permit me to cook or bake. I could wash dishes, vacuum, dust and scour bathrooms, but not cook. So I didn't have the background that most of my peers had. *Yet I was determined to take this on. If Florence could do it, then so could I.*

Needless to say, I had not completed the project by the time my boys woke up. The cookies were baked, but not decorated. So that night, after each of my *"Christmas angels"* was back in bed again, I did the finishing touches on what caused me to feel I'd turned out prize-winning masterpieces. Before baking, I had made holes in the top of each cookie so I could string ribbon through them later. This I did, while my husband Cliff put a tree stand on a very large Douglas fir. This tree would be devoted to the kids in their garage playroom.

Every year, soon after Thanksgiving, we'd visit Jake and Jean, Cliff's cousins in Poulsbo, and their two little girls. The eight of us enjoyed our times together so much during those years, camping and beaching in summer, special times to go crabbing, then feasting, and of course the tree-cutting day. In the 1950's anyone could cut down Douglas firs that grew beneath power lines and not have to pay for them, so we usually brought home several trees to decorate in various rooms of the house.

It took longer than I wanted it to, hanging all those cookies, but did look almost like a picture out of *Better Homes*. Later how I wished I'd taken out my camera. After breakfast next morning, I bundled up the boys so they could play in the backyard and go in and out of their playroom. They were properly impressed once they saw their cookie tree, and solemnly promised no snacking till later. I knew they'd have fun showing off the tree to all their neighborhood chums, chums who were welcome to come through the gate to play, inside or out. My plan was to give each of them a cookie ornament at some point that morning.

As per usual, time raced by too fast as I cleaned up breakfast and neatened the house. As a result, I didn't check on the children soon enough. Maybe you have guessed by now what happened next. But only *part* of your guess would be right. When I opened the door into the playroom to check on how everybody was doing, not a single cookie was left on that tree! Not one, even those up high.

Unbeknownst to me, one of the boys who'd come to play, had brought his very large dog along too. Not one child got even a taste of a cookie. *Only that darn dog!*

I never learned whether my recipe agreed with him.

63

Long Lake Musings

Brilliant
Blue
Green
Brakes*
Sound (a Loon)

Chill
Warmth
Shadow
Sunrays
Cheep (a chipmunk)

Daybreak
Morning passes
Calm
Peace
Celebrate

© 2016, Isabel Jackson

* brakes; thickets of ferns

The Nuts and Bolts of Writing a Villanelle
© 2016, Marilyn White

A villanelle is a poem with specific structure. The poet must carefully choose her pattern, her rhymes, and the lines she wants to repeat plus keep in mind the required metrical beat. Before you write your first villanelle, study other villanelles written by poets before you. "Don't Go Gentle into That Good Night" by Dylan Thomas is an excellent example. Notice the structure and look at the repetitive rhyme pattern carefully. Note there are two lines that repeat according to the pattern throughout the poem, so spend time developing these lines. They will need to fit the required structure, but also flow and make sense as the poem progresses. Note those two repeating lines have a specific place where they need to be inserted in your poem. Establish your two rhyming lines in stanza one. Finally, proofread, workshop, and read your poem for an audience.

Here are the ten basic rules for writing a villanelle:

1. All villanelles must have nineteen lines total. That's it. No more, no less.
2. Every villanelle has only six stanzas.
3. The first five stanzas contain three lines each.
4. The sixth (final) stanza has four lines.
5. There are two rhymes throughout the entire villanelle. For example, in the aforementioned poem by Dylan Thomas, he rhymes *night* and *day*: *night, light, right, bright, flight*, etc. And *day, they, bay, way, pray*, etc. You can see that if you choose words that are easily rhymed, your poem construction will much easier.
6. Line 1 of stanza one is repeated 3 times (the 3rd line in stanzas two, four, and six)
7. Line 3 of stanza one is repeated 3 times (the 3rd line in stanzas three and five, and line four in stanza six).
8. The required rhyming pattern is easier to compose if you think of the two words to be rhymed as 'A' and 'B'. In the Thomas poem night is A, and day is B. In the first five stanzas the

rhyme is consistently: ABA (for example, the final words of the lines are *night, day, light; right, they, night; bright, bay, light, etc.*)

9. Stanza six is slightly different, but no less stringent in the applicable rules. The rhyming pattern of stanza six is ABAA (height, pray, night, light).

10. The final thing to consider—and perhaps the most difficult—is the metrical feet or the beat of each line. Villanelles are acceptable in either tetrameter or pentameter metrical beats. Tetrameter is a line containing four metrical feet (eight beats) that places the stress on every second beat like: daDUM daDUM daDUM daDUM. Pentameter meter is a line containing five metrical feet (ten beats) like: daDUM daDUM daDUM daDUM daDUM, which also places stress on every second beat, but there are a total of ten beats.

I'm not good at this last rule; I can get the ten beats, but the specific daDUM daDUM stress pattern stresses me beyond comfort. After all, I write for pleasure, but it is fun to try to write according to a structure.

That's it. Ready to give it a try? I've written a few villanelles, but here's my favorite: [opposite page]

Favorite Years—A Villanelle

Still young, I enjoyed my favorite years,
Up to bat, I fouled out in fast softball.
Oh slug on; to strike out is my worst fear.

School ends but starts a new book for my peers,
Summer jobs then to college in the fall.
Still young, I enjoyed my favorite years.

I have my choices of many careers,
A wrong selection could be my downfall
Oh slug on; to strike out is my worst fear.

Lawyer, teacher, baker, or financiers?
Alas no career; I wed in the fall.
Still young, I enjoyed my favorite years.

From my honeymoon one choice souvenir,
The wee child in my womb is such a doll.
Oh slug on; to strike out is my worst fear.

Birth, smiles, tears, curfews and big teddy bears,
I declare my daughter's greatest of all.
Still young, I enjoyed my favorite years.
Oh slug on; to strike out is my worst fear.

© 2016, Marilyn White